BEHIND THE NEWS

GLOBAL FINANCIAL CRISIS

Philip Steele

CRABTREE
Publishing Company
www.crabtreebooks.com

Crabtree Publishing Company
www.crabtreebooks.com
1-800-387-7650

Published in Canada
616 Welland Ave.
St. Catharines, ON
L2M 5V6

Published in the United States
PMB 59051, 350 Fifth Ave.
59th Floor,
New York, NY

Published in 2017 by CRABTREE PUBLISHING COMPANY.

First published in 2014 by Wayland
(A division of Hachette Children's Books)
Copyright © Wayland 2014

Author: Philip Steele

Editors: Emma Marriott, Jon Richards, Kathy Middleton, and Janine Deschenes

Designer: Malcolm Parchment

Proofreader: Wendy Scavuzzo

Indexer: Janine Deschenes

**Production coordinator
and prepress technician:** Ken Wright

Print coordinator: Katherine Berti

Photographs and reproductions:
Getty Images: © Charles O'Rear (front cover bottom left); © Stefania Mizara (front cover); © YIORGOS KARAHALIS pp 1, 41, © MAURICIO LIMA p 4; © Justin Sullivan: p 10; © Jeff J Mitchell: p 12; © JONATHAN UTZ: p 14; © Bloomberg: p 22; © CARLOS BARRIA p 34; © Nevada Wier p 36;

Shutterstock: ©Ververidis Vasilis pp 3 (top) 29, 9; ©Kostas Koutsaftikis: pp 3 (bottom right), 29, 40; ©arindambanerjee: p 5; ©Frontpage: p 11; ©meunierd: p 15; ©Glynnis Jones: p 25; ©arindambanerjee: p 26; ©Linda Parton: p 27; ©Lewis Tse Pui Lung: p 35; ©lev radin: p 38; ©1000 Words: p 39; ©joyfull: p42; ©Joseph Sohm: p44

Wikimedia: Cover (bottom right), title page, pp 45, 3, 43, 7, 16, 17, 23, 24, 33

All other images by Shutterstock

Cover: New floor traders learn hand signals at the Chicago Mercantile Exchange (bottom left); Occupy Wall Street protestors (bottom right)

Printed in Canada/072016/PB20160525

Library and Archives Canada Cataloguing in Publication

Steele, Philip, 1948-, author
    Global financial crisis / Philip Steele.

(Behind the news)
Issued in print and electronic formats.
ISBN 978-0-7787-2586-2 (hardback).--
ISBN 978-0-7787-2591-6 (paperback).--
ISBN 978-1-4271-1768-7 (html)

    1. Global Financial Crisis, 2008-2009--Juvenile literature. 2. Financial crises--Juvenile literature. 3. Recessions--Juvenile literature. 4. Economic history--21st century--Juvenile literature. I. Title.

HB3722.S74 2016   j330.9'0511   C2016-902550-0
                                          C2016-902551-9

Library of Congress Cataloging-in-Publication Data

Names: Steele, Philip, 1948- author.
Title: Global financial crisis / Philip Steele.
Description: New York : Crabtree Publishing, 2016. | Series: Behind the news | Includes index.
Identifiers: LCCN 2016016650 (print) | LCCN 2016018469 (ebook) | ISBN 9780778725862 (reinforced library binding) | ISBN 9780778725916 (pbk.) | ISBN 9781427117687 (electronic HTML)
Subjects: LCSH: Global financial crisis, 2008-2009--Juvenile literature. | Financial crises--Juvenile literature.
Classification: LCC HB3722 .S834 2016 (print) | LCC HB3722 (ebook) | DDC 330.9/0511--dc23
LC record available at https://lccn.loc.gov/2016016650

CONTENTS

CRUNCH AND BUST

The 1990s and 2000s were times of great economic change. In the world's most developed countries, jobs in factories and mines were decreasing. Fortunes were now being made in finance, banking, and real estate, or property. Multinational corporations, which are businesses that operate in more than one country, were now richer and more powerful than some nations. In financial centers, such as New York's Wall Street, money still flowed freely.

The big plunge

From 2007 on, the headlines began to tell a very different story. People were unable to make the high payments on their home loans, and the American housing market was in trouble. Banks were going bankrupt, and businesses could not borrow money from the banks that they needed to survive. Unemployment was rising, factory production was falling, and stock markets were diving. The media was using words such as "**credit crunch**," "**downturn**," and

Traders in São Paulo, Brazil, sell dollars on September 15, 2008, the day of the biggest ever bank failure in the United States.

4

"**recession**." A global recession had set in. This led to a financial crisis worldwide, and many countries had to cut back on social services to repay their national debt. People around the world were facing personal financial hardship.

What next?

By 2014, there was hope that a global economic recovery would begin, but many jobs had been lost worldwide, and the standard of living had fallen. The future remains uncertain. Have the problems that started the recession really been fixed, or just covered up? Is a new crisis on the way?

In this book, we go behind the media headlines to find out what went wrong, what was done about it, and whether the solutions worked. We ask whether the current global economic system is fair and if it makes sense. Is the economy stable for years to come or are more **crashes** on the way? In a **globalized** economy, these questions affect everyone on the planet.

THE FALLOUT

- By 2013, house prices in the United States were 30 percent below their high in 2006.
- Between 2007 and 2013, about 20 percent of Americans had lost their jobs at some point. About 25 percent had lost as much as 75 percent of their wealth.
- It was estimated in 2013 that by 2030, nearly 85 percent of working-age adults in the United States will have experienced periods of economic insecurity.

MILESTONES

The financial world has developed over thousands of years, from the days of trading or bartering for goods to the rise of banking in the 1400s. By the 1600s, global trade and the financial institutions we know today were beginning to take shape.

Scottish economist Adam Smith advocated a system of economic self-interest.

• **The first** stock exchange **was founded in Amsterdam in 1602. The Bank of Stockholm in Sweden was issuing banknotes by 1661. Economic "bubbles" became common. Bubbles happen when investors buy stock at highly inflated, unrealistic prices. When the bubble eventually "bursts," the stock collapses in value. A famous** example is the South Sea Company bubble of 1711-20. The company's high-value stocks were reduced to very little. This hurt its** investors.

• **In 1776, Scottish economist Adam Smith wrote that if people pursued wealth for their own benefit, their wealth would in turn create financial benefits for society as a whole. His theories were put to test during the Industrial Revolution, a period of incredible economic growth. His theory laid the foundation for the economic system called** capitalism.

• **In 1846, the German economist Karl Marx publicly disagreed with this system. He declared that capitalism, which is based on the** exploitation **of the workforce, could not be sustained because it benefited only the upper classes.**

During the Great Depression, anxious customers gather in the rain outside the Bank of United States after its failure in 1930.

• After World War I (1914–1918), Germany experienced hyperinflation. By 1923, one American dollar was worth 4,210,500,000,000 German marks (the currency at the time). In 1929, the Wall Street Crash of the American stock market started the Great Depression.

• In the 1930s, English economist John Maynard Keynes said that capitalism could only survive depressions if governments step in by borrowing and spending money to create jobs.

• In 1945, the Bretton Woods Conference in New Hampshire produced an international agreement that established the International Monetary Fund (IMF). It tied international exchange rates to the American dollar, which measured its own value in gold. Called the "gold standard," it lasted until 1971 when the American dollar no longer tied its value to gold.

• In the 1980s, Keynes's ideas of economics were abandoned for the "monetarism" of American economist Milton Friedman. Central banks could print money to meet demand in the market. This was meant to tackle inflation, which was then seen as a larger problem than unemployment. Financial markets had more freedom from government control, and public services became privatized.

• In the 1990s and 2000s, technology was changing the workforce. The Internet was a brand new marketplace, and online businesses exploded. But they quickly became overvalued, and the "dot-com bubble" burst in 2000.

HOW THINGS WENT WRONG

In the 1990s and 2000s, banks were eager for quick profits. Some made risky investments or cut corners. When there was a housing boom, **mortgages** were given to people on low incomes. Few questions were asked as to whether they could afford the monthly repayments. These were called "**subprime**" **loans**.

Toxic debts

From 2004 to 2006, American **interest rates** began to rise sharply. Many people could no longer afford their mortgage payments. Their houses were repossessed, or seized by the banks. Creditors, or the banks that granted the mortgages, took advantage of the situation to make money on the bad debts of homeowners. They sold the homeowners' debts to other banks and investors. These "toxic debts" were extremely harmful to the economy.

Going broke

In 2007, the American subprime mortgage lender New Century Financial went bankrupt. The global **investment bank** Bear Stearns failed, too. Banks ran short of

A notice on a house in the United States shows that this property has been repossessed by the bank after the owner failed to keep up with mortgage payments.

BANK OWNED

NO TRESPASSING

FOR INFORMATION REGARDING THIS PROPERTY OR ANY OTHER BANK-OWNED REAL ESTATE HOLDINGS, PLEASE CONTACT THE FINANCIAL INSTITUTION DIRECTLY AT THIS NUMBER: 561-555-1212

TO VISIT THIS PROPERTY, YOU MAY CONTACT A LICENSED REAL ESTATE BROKER OF YOUR CHOICE. THIS IS A NOTICE OF NON-JUDICIAL FORECLOSURE SALE. THIS IS NOT A TAX SALE OR A SHERIFF SALE. NOTICE IS HEREBY GIVEN TO THE PUBLIC THAT A FINANCIAL INSTITUTION HAS TAKEN OWNERSHIP OF THIS PROPERTY. DO NOT REMOVE THIS NOTICE.

Greeks protest against tax hikes imposed by the central banks in September 2012.

funds themselves and were no longer able to borrow from other banks. In 2008, there were more financial earthquakes. In the United States, Lehman Brothers bank went bankrupt. The United Kingdom's major banks Lloyds TSB, RBS, and HBOS all needed government intervention, or help, to repay their debts.

The house of cards

In Iceland, all three main banks collapsed, leaving their international investors in deep trouble. Ireland's economy took a five-year dive. The European Union (EU), the IMF, and the European Central Bank (ECB) bailed out the Irish economy, but wanted the Irish government to agree to make harsh cuts in its public spending. These cuts are called austerity measures. By 2009, world growth had shrunk to 0.5 percent, the lowest since World War II. World unemployment hit a record high.

A national, or "**sovereign**," debt crisis spread across Europe in countries that used the euro as currency. Spain, Italy, and especially Greece were hit very hard. They relied on central banks to bail them out of debt, but the bailouts had harsh conditions attached, such as agreeing to limits on government spending. In these countries, unemployment soared and protestors took to the streets.

"In my view, the crisis wasn't an accident. We didn't get unlucky. The crisis came because there have been a lot of bad practices and a lot of bad ideas."

David Einhorn, Greenhorn Capital

THE HOME LOANS TRAP, 2008

During the housing boom, finance companies sold mortgages to those who could not afford to pay them back. This practice eventually triggered the global financial crisis. There were probably as many mortgage **foreclosures** in the United States from 2006 to 2013 as there were in total during the Great Depression.

Working with YOU... To Help YOU Achieve Your Goals

This advertisement for mortgage broker Fannie Mae was shown at the 2008 Mortgage Banker's Association.

NEWS FLASH

Date: October 1, 2008
Location: Akron, Ohio
The victim: Addie Polk
The problem: Mortgage foreclosure

A sign of the times

In 2008, Americans were shocked when two government-sponsored enterprises—the Federal National Mortgage Association (known as Fannie Mae) and the Federal Home Loan Mortgage Corporation (known as Freddie Mac)—had to be taken under tight government control. It was a sign that the subprime market had reached crisis point.

The tragedy of Addie Polk

Addie Polk, a woman in her late 80s, took out a mortgage in 2004 with Countrywide

By 2008, the headquarters in Virginia of mortgage-lender Freddie Mac was under state control.

Home Loans on the house she had bought with her late husband, Robert, back in 1970. Addie, a deaconess at her local church, failed to keep up with her mortgage payments. The sheriff's deputies had posted notices of eviction on her door more than 30 times. Her mortgage debt was sold to Fannie Mae, who ordered the house to be foreclosed. Addie was desperate.

Rather than face being removed from her home, Addie tried to shoot herself in the chest. A neighbor found her lying on her bed with a shoulder wound, and she was taken to the hospital. Fannie Mae forgave the debt, but Addie died from an unrelated cause the following spring. She was 91 years old.

Guilty of fraud

In 2013, Countrywide Home Loans was found guilty of **fraud** for selling subprime debts to Fannie Mae and Freddie Mac. The deal had left the two enterprises with a loss of $848 million.

"It appears they're evicting her over her mortgage. She's lived in the house, the neighbors said, something like 38 years and in the last couple of years fell prey to some predatory lending company or financial institution"

Akron police spokesman Lieutenant Rick Edwards (Reuters)

WHO WAS TO BLAME?

In the years before the financial crisis, critics of government economic policies were often dismissed as voices of doom and gloom. So why didn't the economists see it coming? Predicting the behavior of markets and consumers is not an exact science, but had economists just not been thorough or accurate in their analysis?

Money misused?

Who was to blame? Was it the economists, for their lack of foresight? There was a long list of suspects. At the top of the list were the banks and the finance companies. The criticisms directed at them varied from recklessness to carelessness, and from greed to outright fraud. Each of these claims were valid, but was it fair to criticize banking as a whole?

Politics and the public?

Perhaps governments were to blame for overspending and running up their countries' sovereign debt. Had governments failed to properly regulate, or set rules in place for, banks or tackle fraud because they were too eager for financial success? Was it the central banks who were the villains because of misguided policies? Or, were they the

In 2009, the Edinburgh home of Fred Goodwin, former head of RBS, a mismanaged UK bank that was bailed out by taxpayers, was vandalized by protestors who felt those who had mismanaged money had not been punished.

Banks offered easy loans to people wanting to buy pricey household goods, such as cars.

heroes who bailed out sovereign debt and prevented a total meltdown? Were there larger problems with the euro, a new currency introduced across Europe in 1999? Or, was the public to blame?

Many people who made credit card purchases and took on mortgages they could not afford were pointing a finger at the bankers. It is likely many or all of these factors played a part. We have to consider all factors to find out what went wrong, and to stop it from happening again.

> ## "It's not capitalism that has been the problem, but irresponsible governments and politicians who have allowed the financial system to explode by permitting the buildup of ludicrous amounts of debt..."
>
> **Chris Gibson-Smith, chairman of the London Stock Exchange**

DEBATE
Should banks and other financial institutions be more tightly regulated?

YES	NO
Irresponsible and sometimes dishonest management was responsible for the global financial crisis.	*Too many rules and regulations get in the way of business and the creation of wealth.*

THE RISE AND FALL OF PRICES

Could the problem be solved by managing the current economic system better, or does the whole system need reform—or even a revolution? The capitalist system is unstable by nature because money is made by betting on whether markets will rise or fall.

When prices rise...

The capitalist, or free market, system is not as free as it sounds because it is mostly managed by central banks and governments. They try to regulate inflation—the long term rising of the prices of goods and services. If prices rise too quickly, people can no longer afford to purchase goods and services, so company profits fall. If workers are paid more to afford inflated goods, then a company's production costs rise, and the prices it charges for its goods may rise to make up the extra cost. This can kick off a cycle of inflation.

Lastminute.com celebrated its launch in 2000. Within a day, its stock value had risen 34 percent.

DOT-COM BUBBLE

During the dot-com bubble between 1999 and 2001, companies could cause their stock prices to increase by simply adding an "e-" prefix to their name or a ".com" to the end. A combination of circumstances created an environment in which many investors were willing to overlook traditional guidelines in favor of investing in technological advancements.

When prices fall...

If prices become too high, such as during a housing bubble, a crash may follow. People who are paying off home loans may find that they are still paying high rates of interest while the value of their property is actually falling. Because of this, levels of unpaid debts increase.

When prices slide, this is called deflation. People will put off spending cash and buying new goods until the prices stop falling. Fewer sales means companies' profits fall, so the companies lay off workers to reduce their wage costs. This increases unemployment and leads to a decline in the country's gross domestic product (GDP). GDP is the total value of goods produced and services provided within one country over a year. It is a measure of a nation's economic growth or decline. A lack of growth in GDP lasting at least six months in a row is called a recession. Another measure of recession is the level of unemployment.

"The Law of Inflation: Whatever goes up will go up some more."

Anonymous

In 2013, factory workers in Seoul, South Korea, protested against layoffs. The crash following a bubble in one sector, such as housing, can affect the entire economy.

FOUR ECONOMIC THEORIES

Over the centuries, economists have been sharply divided in their views about money, work, production, inflation, unemployment, and social justice, or the fair treatment of citizens. The global financial crisis has focused attention on four economic thinkers in particular.

Adam Smith (1723–1790)

Known as the father of economics, Adam Smith valued **commercial** competition and believed that self-interest worked for the greater good of all. Smith called for free, unregulated markets. He believed that if markets were left to themselves, they would achieve a natural balance.

Smith believed free markets made societies fairer. Yet extreme inequalities have arisen in modern markets.

Karl Marx (1818–1883)

Karl Marx said that capitalism was unjust and unsustainable. He described how capitalists own and control the production of goods and services, and therefore make a profit off them. He believed that this takes advantage of the working-class people who produce the goods. According to Marx, profit should belong to the workers. He believed social progress would only come from the working class resisting exploitation by capitalists.

Keynes felt unemployment could reduce demand so much that no jobs could be created.

John Maynard Keynes (1883–1946)

John Maynard Keynes was a capitalist who helped to plan the **World Bank** and the International Monetary Fund. He had foreseen the dangers of hyperinflation and the Great Depression in the 1920s and 1930s. He believed that governments had a duty to take control of the economy and reduce unemployment through **fiscal policy**, or taxes and spending. He did not trust the markets to regulate themselves.

Milton Friedman (1912–2006)

Milton Friedman believed that governments should only be involved in controlling the amount and price of money in the economy. His theory is called monetarism. Since the 1980s, many governments were influenced by his ideas. They deregulated, or removed government controls, from banks and financial services, and encouraged free markets. They also transferred public services into private ownership, a process called privatization.

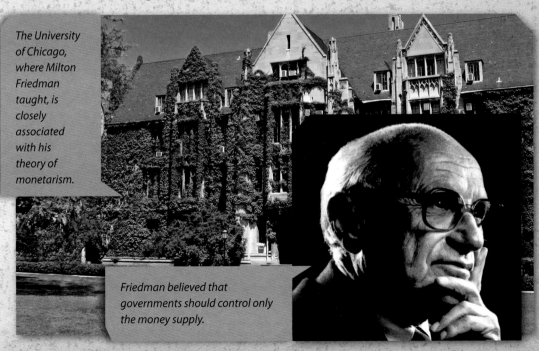

The University of Chicago, where Milton Friedman taught, is closely associated with his theory of monetarism.

Friedman believed that governments should control only the money supply.

HOW SECURE IS OUR MONEY?

Is the global economic system of the 21st century built on shaky foundations? Are financial crises the result of ongoing flaws in methods of economic management or policy?

"In the absence of the gold standard, there is no way to protect savings from confiscation [being taken away] through inflation. There is no safe store of value."

Alan Greenspan, Chairman of the US Federal Reserve

For much of the 20th century, the value of currency was tied to a fixed quantity of gold.

Made-up money

Some economists trace problems back to the end of the Bretton Woods agreement in 1971, when the American dollar and the world's major currencies were no longer related to any gold standard (see page 7). Without the gold standard, the value of money was deregulated, meaning government controls were removed. Governments and central banks could decide the value of money, and print more money whenever needed. This practice, however, causes inflation, which can decrease the value of savings because money saved today has less spending power in a future where prices are higher.

Inflation and growth

Governments need to prevent serious inflation spirals in which rising wages encourage rising prices. But governments also have to maintain some low level of inflation to keep the economy growing. The crucial question is how much growth do we all actually need? Is growth the correct measure of success? On a planet with limited resources, can continuous growth go on forever?

Friedman's failure?

In the 1980s, many nations gave up on the fiscal approaches of Keynes, in which governments intervened to create jobs. Instead they followed the policies of Milton Friedman by reducing government intervention and letting market forces rule the day. The strategy was to limit **labor union** powers and workers' rights, to cut the workforce, and increase productivity. These steps made companies more profitable, and people who invested in them had higher returns. Banks and financial institutions were free from regulations that held back huge profits.

Some people believe that the 2008 recession was the final proof that the Friedman experiment had failed—yet, others still think it is a long-term solution.

Friedman's system is associated with high-risk, high-reward banking known as "casino capitalism."

"**By a continuing process of inflation, governments can confiscate, secretly and unobserved, an important part of the wealth of their citizens.**"

John Maynard Keynes

THE PROBLEMS WITH BANKS

We use the word "bank" to describe all sorts of institutions. A central bank is a financial hub which controls national interest rates and manages the money supply. Investment banks provide financial services, while retail banks deal with everyday transactions, savings, and personal or business loans.

Emergency measures

As the global financial crisis tightened its grip, central banks took various measures to halt the recession. One remedy was called **quantitative easing** (QE). Central banks tried to stimulate the economy by increasing the quantity of money available. They did this by buying long-term **bonds**, or other **financial instruments** that had value, from banks and other financial institutions. These purchases loaned money to the banks, so that they could have enough money to loan to businesses. When businesses have more money, the economy can grow. As a policy, QE needed careful balancing. Too much

The policy of quantitative easing means that banks will print more money to prevent any fall in the money supply.

easing could cause hyperinflation. Not enough, and the banks might refuse to lend money to businesses. Did it work? Some say it had little impact, but the IMF felt that it did prove to be worthwhile.

Too much power?

After 2009, as the sovereign debt crisis spread throughout Europe, central banks bailed out entire countries, imposing extremely harsh conditions in return for massive transfers of money. This averted disaster, but revealed just how much power central banks now held over national governments. As independent institutions, central banks were not accountable to the public and had no democratic rules. Is capitalism really about freedom, as Friedman claimed, or is it really just controlled by international bankers?

Teachers in Greece demonstrated against the job cuts demanded by the country's international creditors in 2012. Greece was hit especially hard by austerity measures, or spending and budget cuts.

"We have suffered dramatic wage cuts...But we are not fighting for money or privileges... We are fighting to save education."

Thomai Pagiantza, teacher at an elementary school in Alexandria, northern Greece

LEHMAN BROTHERS, 2008

It was said that Lehman Brothers bank was too big to fail. After all, it was the fourth-largest investment bank in the United States. It had a long track record of success having survived the Wall Street Crash of 1929 and the Great Depression of the 1930s.

NEWS FLASH

Date: September 15, 2008
Locations: New York City and global
The firm: Lehman Brothers Holdings Inc.
The boss: Richard S. Fuld Jr.
The problem: Bankruptcy

Richard S. Fuld Jr., the CEO of Lehman Brothers, was known on Wall Street as "the Gorilla" for his aggressive style.

Going down in flames

In the years 2003 to 2005, Lehman Brothers bought five mortgage-lending companies, including a subprime mortgage lender. They made record profits—until the housing market fell apart. In 2008, the five companies failed, and the value of Lehman shares, or parts of the company owned by people called shareholders, fell by 42 percent. The United States government decided not to bail them out, forcing the company, which had over $600 billion in debt, to file for the largest bankruptcy in American history. Approximately 26,000 employees lost their jobs. Streams of anxious men and women left their offices, clutching boxes with their personal possessions.

A group of subprime mortgage failures left Lehman Brothers with debts far larger than what the company was worth.

The crash effect

The Lehman Brothers crash affected investors around the world and hit other major banks, such as HBOS, the United Kingdom's biggest mortgage lender. The stock market became highly unstable, confirming that this was a crisis on an epic scale. The United States government had to change its mind about bailouts as financial institutions struggled.

Bonus bonanza

The fall of Lehman Brothers gave banking a bad name. It was soon discovered that the company had been using dishonest accounting to conceal its massive debts. Meanwhile, senior Lehman executives had left with huge payouts. It was revealed that, in the year before the bankruptcy, the Chief Executive Officer (CEO) Richard Fuld had earned a basic salary of $750,000, plus a cash bonus of $4,250,000, plus stock worth $16,877,365—while his former employees struggled, jobless in a recessive economy.

"Your company is now bankrupt, our economy is in a state of crisis, but you get to keep $480 million. I have a very basic question for you: Is this fair?"

US Representative for California Henry Waxman (Democrat), to Lehman CEO Richard Fuld

RESPONDING TO CRISIS

Critics argued that the reckless pursuit of profit by investment bankers was at the heart of the crisis. The bankers borrowed money to buy more **assets**, hoping that the money made from the assets would rise faster than the cost of buying them. This process, which uses loans for company spending, is called leverage. Too much leverage, however, puts company profits at risk.

"The government bailed out the people and imprisoned the banksters—the opposite of what America and the rest of Europe did."

Ólafur Ragnar Grímsson, President of Iceland

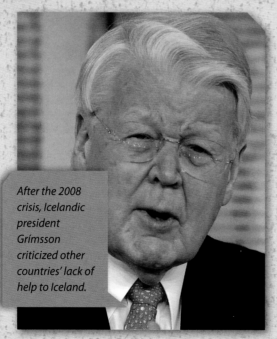

After the 2008 crisis, Icelandic president Grímsson criticized other countries' lack of help to Iceland.

How did governments respond?

Governments temporarily took control or ownership of some troubled banks. This meant that they could use public money to help the banks and restructure them so that everyday transactions would be separate from the bad debts. Iceland, on the other hand, let its big banks go bankrupt and refused to pay their debts. This policy was praised by financial commentators.

Bash the bankers?

Public opinion was already infuriated by the high salaries and bonuses of the bankers. Many people became even angrier when

Public backlash against the banks' behavior grew in 2011. Here, protestors walk past the New York Stock Exchange in July, 2012.

taxpayers' money was used to bail out the banks. In 2010, President Barack Obama signed the Dodd-Frank Act into law, which regulates Wall Street business in a way that protects the public. Among the new regulations are those that limit bonuses and end taxpayer-funded bailouts.

Financial crime

So was the crisis really due to too much leverage and pursuit of profit? Or, did the problem go deeper? Some banks had been engaging in false accounting, or fraud. In 2012, it was discovered that some banks had schemed to set the London Interbank Offered Rate (LIBOR)—

the interest rate for lending and borrowing—artificially low. Since the rate is set by banks reporting the interest rates they would have to pay if they borrowed from one another, the banks reported paying interest rates that were actually lower than what they paid. This way, they could make profit from large investments with lower interest rates. This might have affected trillions of dollars' worth of business in the United States. While there were calls for more severe punishments for financial crime in the United Kingdom, the American system was more prepared to jail fraudsters.

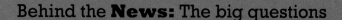

SHOULD BAILOUTS BE GIVEN?

The global recession meant that consumers had less money to spend. This hit many major American companies extremely hard—though none may have crashed as hard as the North American automobile industry. With more debt than they were worth, some companies faced bankruptcy. They turned to the government to bail them out.

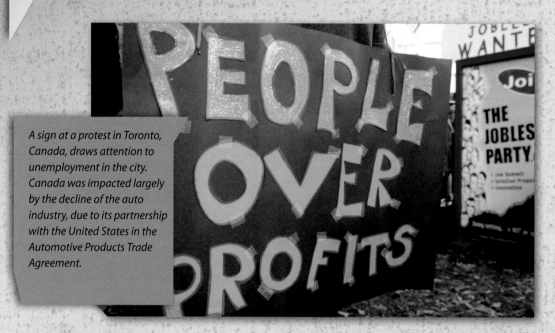

A sign at a protest in Toronto, Canada, draws attention to unemployment in the city. Canada was impacted largely by the decline of the auto industry, due to its partnership with the United States in the Automotive Products Trade Agreement.

The auto industry

The global recession meant that fewer people could afford to buy cars. Rising oil prices in 2008 were also making it more expensive for companies to make cars and for consumers to buy gasoline to power them. America's Big Three auto companies—Ford, Chrysler, and General Motors—had specialized in producing large vehicles such as SUVs and trucks. More expensive to buy, they also used more gas, making them unaffordable.

To make up for the drop in car sales, the Big Three made cuts to employee benefits, borrowed large amounts of money, shut down car dealerships, and even laid off employees. The effects of the auto industry downturn were felt across the United States and Canada. In 2009, the US government spent more than $80 billion and the Candian government more than $13 billion to bail out the Big Three, to keep them from collapse and save approximately two million jobs.

In hot water

A bailout is financial assistance given to keep a company from collapse. The United States government also made other expensive bailouts. Large banks were bailed out to keep as many citizens as possible from losing their savings. The bailouts were praised by some commentators, but others questioned why large companies were allowed to stay afloat while many individual citizens had lost their jobs, homes, and savings. Many people also criticized the government for using taxpayer money to fund the bailouts.

Shown are the headquarters of General Motors in Detroit, Michigan. The company declared bankruptcy in June 2009, following Chrysler's declaration in April—a company also headquartered in Detroit. The city was hit very hard by the decline of the auto industry, and declared its own bankruptcy in July 2013.

> ## "The Federal Reserve must be reformed to serve the needs of working families, not just CEOs on Wall Street."
>
> Bernie Sanders, American politician, 2011

DEBATE
Should governments bail out banks and large corporations?

YES

Large corporations are essential in keeping the economy going. Allowing them to collapse would make the economy worse, and many more people would lose their jobs.

NO

Taxpayers should not have to pay for the mistakes of big corporations. Mismanaged companies should be allowed to fail, and governments should only help struggling citizens.

INTRODUCING AUSTERITY

The financial crisis had caused hardship around the world. With the sovereign debt crisis in Europe, the IMF, the European Central Bank, the European Union (a membership of 28 countries in Europe), and many other national governments all adopted austerity measures. But does austerity do more harm than good?

Kill or cure?

Economic austerity means a severe cutback in public spending by central, regional, or local government. Severe austerity cuts were made across southern Europe and in Ireland during the financial crisis, and to a lesser degree in the USA.

In the United Kingdom, the aim was to reduce the rate at which the government borrowed money. The difference between government income and spending, or the amount of debt a government has, is called the budget deficit. Ongoing austerity policies aimed at national deficit

GREEK UNEMPLOYMENT RATE, BY AGE GROUP, OCTOBER 2007–2012 (%)

AGE GROUP	2007	2008	2009	2010	2011	2012
15–24	22.9	22.1	28.5	34.7	46.7	56.6
25–34	11.6	10.6	13.0	18.9	27.0	34.1
35–44	6.3	6.1	8.3	11.6	15.9	23.3
45–54	4.5	4.5	6.9	9.3	14.2	19.5
55–64	3.1	3.1	4.9	6.8	9.0	15.4
65–74	1.4	0.8	1.0	1.9	3.6	4.9
Total	8.1	7.5	10	13.8	19.7	26.8

Source: Greek Statistical Authority, January 2013

Austerity measures in Greece led to violent social unrest. Young protestors hurled stones at police in Athens in 2008.

reduction involved privatizing public services, introducing or increasing fees for services, and reforming the system to make it harder for people to claim unemployement **benefits** for unemployment or disability.

Where's the catch?

Critics of austerity measures feared that cutting public services would slow the recovery of businesses. For example, if library services were cut, publishers would sell fewer books. If fire departments were cut, then firefighting equipment companies would become less profitable. Workers would then lose their jobs and need to claim unemployment benefits, which is another cost to the government. Some opponents felt the targets of the cuts were chosen for political reasons. For example, people questioned why hospitals were closed or cuts were made to education, while expensive nuclear weapons programs were fully funded.

"**The situation that the workers are undergoing is tragic and we are near poverty levels.**"

Greek trade unionist Spyros Linardopoulos, interviewed by the BBC

SHOULD WE SPEND OR SAVE?

The big political debate has been waged over whether austerity actually works. Some say it is just common sense. Isn't attacking the budget deficit really a question of balancing the books? Some argue that using austerity cuts to reduce debt is a good idea.

"It is absolutely possible to have fiscal consolidation and growth at the same time. It's a big discussion topic: must we always get into debt for growth? We have proved in the last years that we don't have to."

Angela Merkel, German Chancellor

To cut or not to cut?

Followers of the economist John Maynard Keynes believe austerity programs should only be put in place if an economy is at a time of strong growth. During a slump, the government should be spending its way out of debt. Public spending creates jobs, which means people have more money to spend on goods. This spending helps businesses, which boosts the economy and helps it expand. Then, Keynesian economists argue, governments can begin reducing spending and borrowing.

Better times ahead?

So, which side of the debate—for or against austerity—seems to be winning? Economic forecasts had some good news for austerity supporters. Retail sales were rising more than expected, and claims for unemployment benefits were falling. Growth forecasts were up, and factories were reporting higher demands for their goods.

But was this a direct result of the austerity cuts? The Bank of England pointed out that recovery in the United Kingdom, where austerity measures had

The Hoover Dam (built from 1931–1936) was one of the vast building projects of the United States New Deal—the spending plan that helped boost the economy out of the Great Depression.

> ## "It is deeply destructive to pursue austerity in a depression."

Paul Krugman, Nobel prize winning economist

been imposed, was far behind recovery in the United States, where austerity measures had been less extreme. Some economists said that low interest rates were fueling a possible recovery, and that the government had been spending more than it had planned. Is it possible that any recovery might have been stronger without austerity cuts being imposed in the first place?

DEBATE   Does austerity work?

YES
Cutting wasteful spending and reducing the deficit is necessary to get the economy back to good health.

NO
Cutting jobs reduces spending power and drives the economy back into recession.

THE GLOBAL IMPACT

Countries around the world felt the impact of the recession. Even in the "BRICS" countries (named for the first letters of Brazil, Russia, India, China, and South Africa), where growth rates had been breaking records, a slow-down had begun. As exports fell, China tried to shift its focus from exports to the home market.

Going worldwide

Exports, or goods sold to customers outside the country, also fell in Africa as international demand began to drop off. There were fears that international aid budgets for some countries would be cut.

The Japanese economy had already experienced its own problems of **stagnation** and recession ever since the early 1990s, and the global recession made recovery harder. Australia seemed to weather the storm, perhaps because of its huge iron ore wealth or the fiscal policies of its Reserve Bank. Similarly, the

The building boom in China continued, without slowing down, as the state encouraged consumerism, or the buying of goods.

Golden Dawn, Greece's far-right party, demonstrate outside the Greek parliament building in 2013. Riding on a wave of public resentment towards the EU, the party won three seats in the 2014 European Elections.

Canadian economy was not affected as severely as that of its southern neighbor. However, the country fell officially into a recession in 2008. Canadian exports of resources—an important part of the country's economy—were weakened.

Euro panic

For the **Eurozone** nations, the financial crisis had the impact of a tsunami. Some countries were already loaded with bad sovereign debt and were in no position to bail out their failing banks and companies.

Private credit rating companies rate the credits of sovereign nations based on how reliable they would be to pay back their debt. The ratings had a lot of influence on whether nations could continue borrowing money to keep their economies afloat. During that time, the credit rating companies had a lot of power because a bad rating could send a national economy into turmoil. Only the intervention of the IMF, the European Union (EU), and the European Central Bank (ECB) could help, but the austerity measures they imposed were too extreme.

By mid 2013, unemployment in Greece and Spain had soared to 27 percent. Resentment grew against the wealthier northern nations, such as Germany, which were demanding that their southern neighbors enact strict austerity measures.

Political consequences

Political turmoil led to abrupt changes of government across the region and damaged the stability of the EU. Mario Monti, a leading economist, was appointed Italian prime minister to head a team of unelected "experts" to sort out the mess. In Greece, members of a **far-right** party were elected to parliament. Would democracy survive the recession?

LAYOFFS, CHINA, 2008

Although China is still governed by the Communist Party, it had moved from **communist** economics to a form of capitalism controlled by the government. Growth had soared, but took a dip in 2008 and 2009 because of the worldwide recession. Times became very tough for low-paid workers in China.

NEWS FLASH

Year: 2008
Locations: Shandong, Hubei, and Guangdong provinces, People's Republic of China
The problem: Effect of the recession on Chinese exports
Outcomes: Factory closures, job losses

A man walks past a closed factory in Wenzhou, Zhejiang Province, in 2011 after the bankruptcy of the owner.

No exports, no work

Chinese New Year, or Spring Festival, is a time when many Chinese working people like to go home to visit their families. City railway stations are full of **migrant workers** carrying bags full of gifts to take back to their villages in the countryside. However, in 2008, many were leaving the cities on a one-way ticket. Factories in the big cities were closing down. Because of the recession, overseas markets were no longer importing, or bringing in, as many Chinese goods.

In 2008, tens of thousands of small

As growth slowed in China, workers returned to small, family-owned businesses like this one in Puning, Guangdong Province.

firms closed down in the southern province of Guangdong. Even if factories stayed open, some workers had to accept a 75 percent cut in wages. In some cases, the government stepped in with financial support for laid-off workforces.

China, on the up or down?

Growth did recover in China, which today has the world's second largest economy after the United States. In 2013, the Chinese government said it was prepared to have a lower growth rate, and rely more on increasing sales of goods and services within China than on the export markets. Big economic and social reforms were brought in, with greater reliance on market forces and a movement away from government control. Was this a recipe for success or disaster? Some economists predicted success for the project, but international financier George Soros warned that a rise in Chinese debt could open a whole new chapter in the global financial crisis.

"One day we went to work as usual, the next it was all closed. Thousands of us are looking for jobs now. We walk around every day till our feet ache but we can't find anything."

Migrant worker Wei Sunying, a former toy factory employee in Dongguan, *The Guardian*, 2008

IS GLOBALIZATION THE ANSWER?

The International Monetary Fund promotes economic cooperation between countries; the World Bank loans money to developing nations; and the World Trade Organization (WTO) regulates international trade. Perhaps the ultimate symbol of the global market is the Internet, which allows global trading at lightning speeds.

Globalization—a blessing or a curse?

Was globalization—the worldwide merging together of markets and trade—a factor in the crisis? Economies around the world are now so interconnected, if one falls, they all go down like dominoes. The downturn certainly seemed to prove the saying, "If America sneezes, the whole world catches a cold," describing the large impact the United States has on the world economy. Global trade often means that the goods we use are brought in from other countries. However, if there is unemployment and recession in the United States, does it make sense to move jobs to Bangalore in India, where labor is cheaper? Supporters believe globalization creates wealth, encourages development, and stabilizes economies, because it can create jobs and companies can transport goods around the world.

With improved communications technology, companies can now base their customer service centers in places where labor costs are cheaper.

On the other hand, critics say that global wealth gets distributed unequally between countries, and financial interests are often placed above human rights, as in the case of child labor, or the environment.

Barriers to free trade?

The recession has threatened global trade in many ways. New regulations require banks to increase their access to money to reduce future risk, making it harder for them to finance international trade. Some politicians talk about protecting national markets by introducing restrictive trade measures. This policy is called **protectionism** and is resisted by the WTO, which insists that free trade is the best route out of recession.

Improvements in transportation have been a major driver in globalization. The United States has invested in this "mega-port" in Shanghai, China, making it the largest shipping port in the world. It handles more than 700 million tons of cargo every year.

DEBATE

Should it matter that our goods are made in foreign countries?

YES
In hard times, countries should look after the interests of their own workers.

NO
The world has moved on from that position. Free trade works best when it is global.

POVERTY AND JUSTICE

The debate about the global financial crisis is often a fierce one. Many different arguments are raised. Most of these theories talk about eradicating poverty and promoting social justice, yet propose completely different economic and social solutions.

On one hand...

Adam Smith (see page 6) wrote that self-interest acts in the interest of the common good. Many politicians today believe that giving individuals an equal opportunity to succeed is better than using taxes to redistribute wealth to

people more evenly. They believe that the rich boost the economy by spending money, which creates jobs. In this way, wealth "trickles down" to less wealthy people. They also argue that the chance of earning money makes others aspire to do the same. According to this viewpoint,

Volunteers are shown distributing food at a food bank in New York in 2010 to people unable to feed their families.

welfare and the expectation of benefits only rewards laziness and comes at a cost too high for an economy in recession. Private firms can do the same job public services do, but more efficiently because they have to compete with other companies.

... but on the other hand

Those who oppose this argument might point out that **taxation** is used to make society fairer for all. At the moment, equal opportunities are only a dream, since the possibility for financial success is unequally affected by many factors including geography, race, and social or economic situations. They believe "self-interest" breeds greed. Wherever neo-liberal policies (see page 19) have been used, the result has been a sharp increase in the **poverty gap**. This increases problems such as social unrest, poor health, or crime. Social welfare programs can be affordable and provide an essential safety net for citizens, which is especially important in times of recession. Those who support this viewpoint argue that cutting public services appears to save money in the beginning, but is much more costly down the road. Privatized firms serve the interest of shareholders rather than the public.

DEBATE

Should the tax system redistribute wealth to the disadvantaged?

YES
In a civilized society, fiscal policy should be used to protect the poorest from hardship.

NO
The tax system should be there to reward and encourage economic opportunity, not to give handouts.

SOCIAL ISSUES, GREECE, 2008-2016

Since 2008, it is estimated that Greece has received over 300 billion euros ($340 billion US) in loans from the IMF, ECB, and EU, but in that period the economy has shrunk by 23 percent. Unemployment is still over 25 percent. Whatever caused this situation, it was the Greek people who were blamed for the crisis and who paid the price.

NEWS FLASH

Date: 2008-2016
Location: Greece
The problem: Sovereign debt crisis
Measures imposed: Severe austerity
Outcome: Social breakdown

Tempers ran high outside the Greek parliament building in 2011 as protestors vented their feelings against the EU's austerity measures.

Austerity catastrophe

The word "catastrophe" comes from the ancient Greek language. It means an overturning, a sudden end, or a fatal turning point. For modern Greeks, the catastrophic economic figures above meant austerity measures were imposed on them to an extent usually only seen during wartime. Taxes were increased on income, property, purchases, and fuel. Public sector jobs were cut and wages slashed. Health spending was cut by

billions of euros. Closures or mergers were planned for 1,976 schools. Teachers' salaries were cut by about 40 percent. The state pension age was raised, and welfare benefits were cut.

Jobless Greeks line up outside an employment office in 2011. In that year, unemployment reached 18 percent—up 48 percent over the previous year.

The social cost

Suicide rates rose by about 40 percent in the first five months of 2011. In 2012, the minimum wage was cut by 22 percent. Charities have had to supply free food parcels. Families have suffered. Prisons have become run down and overcrowded as budgets were cut. And if austerity has been making things bad for the Greeks, it has been even worse for penniless migrants and refugees who have entered Greece from Africa or the Middle East, fleeing wars or even worse poverty. Migrants were blamed for Greece's troubles and often attacked on the street by frustrated citizens.

In August 2015, Eurozone finance ministers agreed to bail out Greece a third time, committing to lending the struggling country 86 billion euros ($97 billion US) over three years. Could the country stay in recession for more years to come?

> "The crisis has made a bad situation worse. Alcoholism, drug abuse, and psychiatric problems are on the rise, and more and more children are being abandoned on the streets."
>
> Costas Yannopoulos, from the charity Smile of the Child, *The Guardian*, 2011

WHAT IS THE ANSWER?

Throughout history, politicians and business leaders have often caused great human suffering by implementing all kinds of extreme economic plans. To avoid criticism, they would manipulate facts in the media to fit their ideas. However, these economic plans are doomed to fail because they are not sustainable on a human level.

Children scavenge for food at a garbage bin in Ukraine in 2009. The country has about 50,000 children living on the streets.

The human factor

Economic theories may crunch numbers and talk about inflation, leverage, supply, and demand—but these words and theories often ignore the human factor. Recession, unemployment, and debt can have devastating effects on people's lives. Did the bankers and financial CEOs think through the consequences of their actions? Economics should always be matched to human need. After all, do we want money to work for us or enslave us?

Predatory lending

Making money by charging sky-high interest rates on loans to vulnerable people, such as through "payday" loans, have become a notorious feature of the financial crisis. Payday loan companies offer short-term credit to those in immediate need of money, sometimes attached to an annual interest rate of more than 1,000 percent. This way, the companies profit off the plight of those in need.

Speaking out—Occupy Wall Street

A response to the global financial crisis, the Occupy movement speaks out against large corporations and banks that engage in financial practices that harm the public. The first Occupy protest, Occupy Wall Street, gained a great amount of attention when it demonstrated in New York City in 2011. The group spoke out against the practices of companies on Wall Street, arguing that the immense gap in wealth between the rich and everyone else is proof that the American economy benefits the rich above others. The highest 1 percent of American earners hold a high, unequal percentage of the country's total wealth. Representing the remaining "99 percent," the Occupy movement pushes for social and economic equality around the world.

> **"Nowadays people know the price of everything and the value of nothing."**
>
> **Oscar Wilde, *The Picture of Dorian Gray*, 1890**

BETTING ON FUTURES

The global financial crisis made many people feel a sense of great injustice. Why should the poor suffer because of mistakes made by millionaire bankers? At a time when the public were being asked to make great sacrifices, why were vastly rich multinational companies being allowed to pay less tax?

> "As long as the problems of the poor are not radically resolved by rejecting the absolute autonomy of markets and financial speculation, and by attacking the structural causes of inequality, no solution will be found for the world's problems..."
>
> **Pope Francis, head of the Roman Catholic Church.**

The debate goes on

By 2014, it seemed that a recovery might take hold—at least in the United States. Had the crisis at last been resolved? Would the public concern now evaporate?

British Chancellor, George Osborne, was quick to point out that many more years of austerity cuts in Europe were still to come. It seems that heated debate, for and against cuts, is likely to continue.

Migrant workers arrive to pick crops in California, just as they did during the Great Depression of the 1930s.

Dorothea Lange's famous photograph taken during the Great Depression captures the despair on the face of a migrant worker.

New writers are arguing that inequality prevents a country from running efficiently. But do politicians agree? The gap between rich and poor grows wider.

Have the problems been fixed?

Concern has been expressed by many economists that the lessons of the global financial crisis have not been learned. For example, student textbooks need to be revised to include the financial crisis, or show some of the differing opinions on economic policy. We need to learn about that crisis to avoid another. A novel called *The Way We Live Now* describes how greed and dishonesty can take hold of the financial system at great social cost. That book was written by Anthony Trollope— back in 1873! Are we doomed to repeat past mistakes, or can the globalized world now look forward to a brighter future?

A changing world

The answer to that question will depend on many unknowns. Economic change will be affected by factors such as technological advances, population growth or decline, resources, climate and environment, and political stability. Ultimately, no new economic plan will work if it is not accountable to the people whose lives it affects. Economists and politicians often bet on the prices of future economic goods to make profits. It is important that we understand they are betting on all of our futures.

GLOSSARY

assets
Property owned that has value in money

benefit
A payment or other assistance intended to help members of society in need

bonds
Loans from banks, governments, or organizations that are bought by the public for a fixed amount of time

bubble
An economic crisis caused by overvalued stocks and unsustainable prices

capitalism
An economic system based on the accumulation of money, private ownership, competition, and wage labor

central bank
A national institution that may manage currency, money supply, and regulation

commercial
Having to do with a system of commerce, business, or profit

communist
A system in which goods and property is commonly, rather than privately, owned

crash
The sudden, disastrous collapse of a market, as in the Wall Street Crash of 1929

credit crunch
A sudden reduction in the availability of credit, or loans, from banks and lenders

depression
A long period of economic decline or recession, sometimes defined as lasting for two years or more

downturn
A decline in economic activity or profit

Eurozone
The group of 19 European nations, including France, Germany, and Greece, which have adopted the Euro as currency

exploitation
Treating someone unfairly to benefit from their work

financial instruments
A legal document representing a type of monetary value, such as bonds

fiscal policy
Government policy that deals with taxation and spending

foreclosure
An attempt by a lender to recover the balance of a bad debt; for example, a bank may seize a home if its purchaser cannot keep up mortgage repayments

fraud
Financial deception and corruption

globalize
Integrate economics worldwide with international corporations, rapid communications, and the movement of money and labor across borders

gold standard
A monetary system in which the currency is based on a fixed value in gold

hyperinflation
A dangerously high and rapidly increasing rate of inflation

interest rate

The rate at which interest on borrowed money has to be paid to the lender

International Monetary Fund

An international organization including 188 countries, which work together to standardize global financial relations

investor

Someone who buys an asset or item with the hope that it will make them profit

investment bank

A bank that helps people, companies, or other banks to raise money

labor union

An organization of workers that aims to protect working standards, employment, wages, and working conditions

layoffs

The laying off of workers

market

A group of buyers (demand) and sellers (supply) and the means or space in which they exchange goods and services

migrant worker

A person who moves from place to place, often internationally, to find work

monetarism

A policy that focuses on money supply

mortgage

A loan used to buy property, secured against the value of that property

neo-liberal

Relating to a form of liberalism that favors free-market capitalism

poverty gap

A measurement of poverty, defined based on the minimum income needed to live

privatize

Turn publicly owned services over to private ownership

protectionism

Regulating free international trade to support businesses in one country

quantitative easing

A way of stimulating the economy during a financial crisis; a central bank buys assets, such as stocks and bonds, from commercial banks so that they can lend more money

recession

A period of decline in trade and industry, lasting two months or more

sovereign debt

Government debt, which is used to finance growth; repayment may become difficult in a financial crisis

stagnation

A prolonged period of little to no growth in the economy

stock exchange

A market in which bonds, company shares, and other assets are bought and sold

subprime lending

High-risk loans made to people who may have trouble with repayment

taxation

The imposition of charges payable to the state, due on private income, services, property, or trade; taxes are used to fund public works, services, and welfare

World Bank

An international bank in which nations have membership; the World Bank provides loans to developing countries

INDEX